This book belongs to:

If You Were A Jelly Bean

written by Dodd Ferrelle
illustrated by Cameron Bliss Ferrelle

For Dodd, Bliss and Lucas. We love you!
You all are our favorites!

Get your FREE DOWNLOAD of the song My Favorite and sing along with the book !
https://thehappyhandsband.bandcamp.com/track/my-favorite

If you were a jelly bean

you would be a ________

jelly bean, because

that is my favorite!

If you were an animal
you would be a ______,
because that is my favorite!

If you were a fruit
because that is

you would be a __________ ,
my favorite!

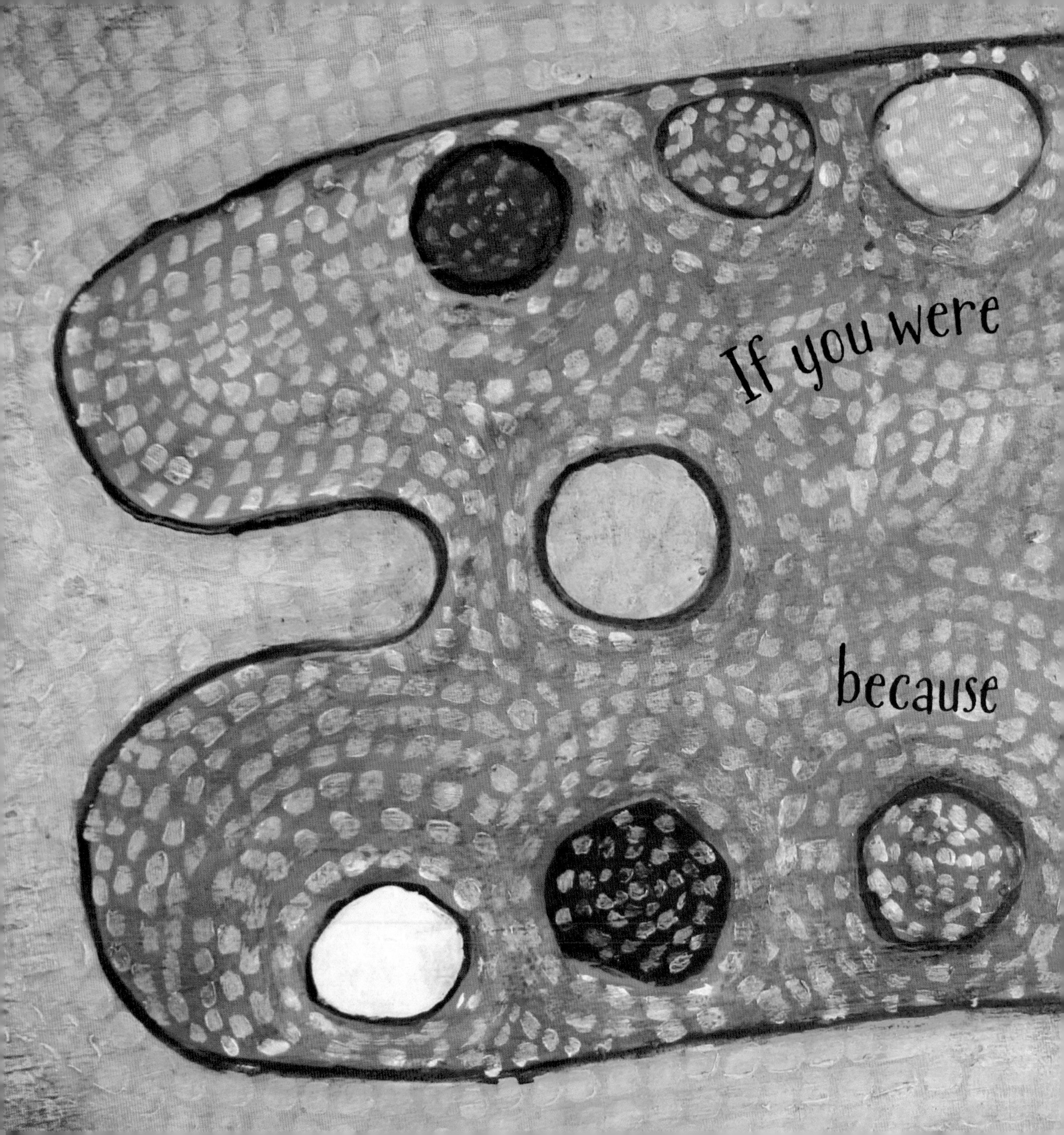

If you were

because

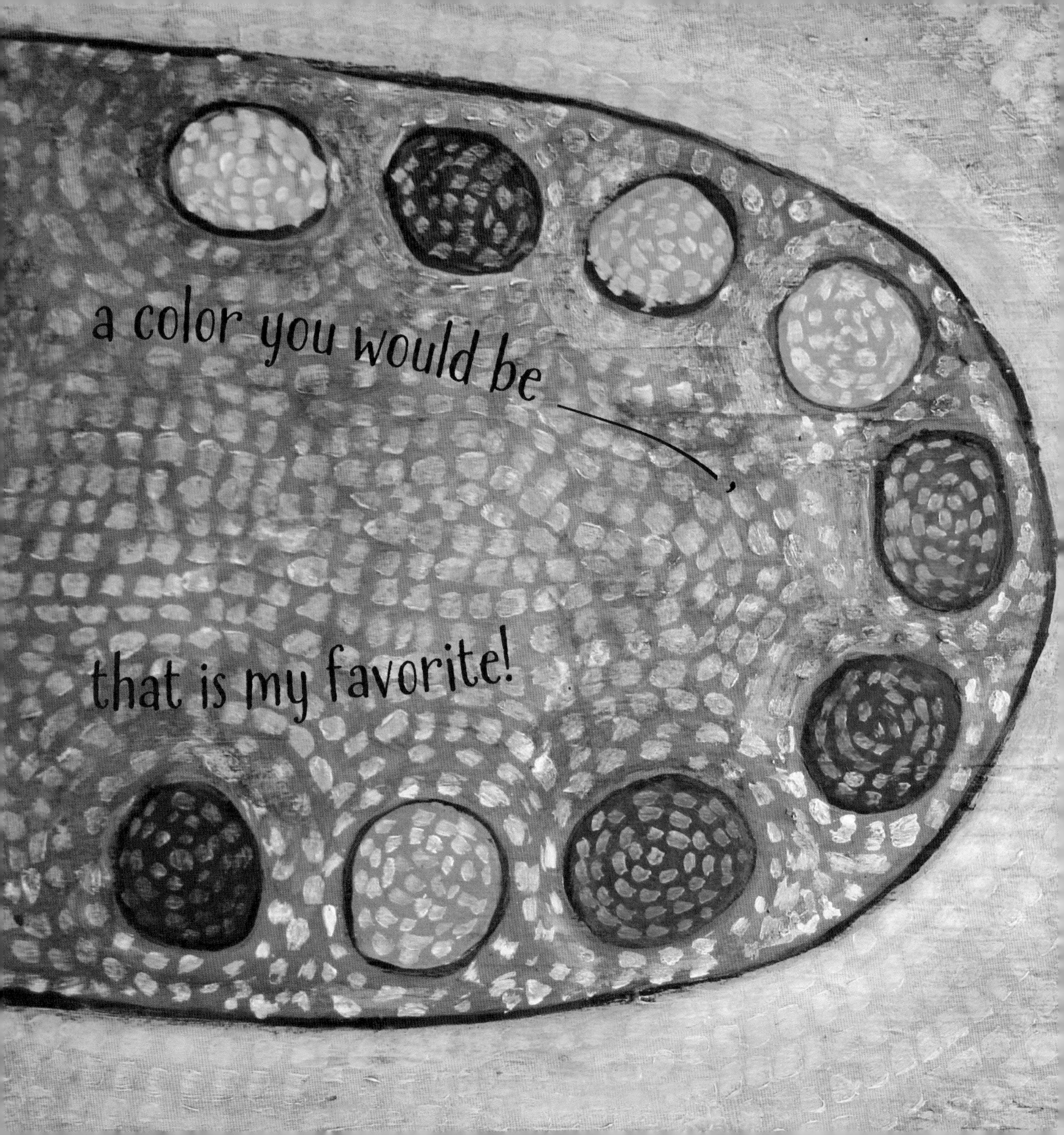
a color you would be ______,
that is my favorite!

If you were an instrument
because that is

you would be a ______,
my favorite!

Wednesday
Tuesday
If you were a day of the
because that is
Monday
Friday

week you would be ________,

my favorite!

If you were a season you would be

_______ because that is my favorite!

2
L
D
7
B
6

If you were a toy
you would be a __________,
because that is
my favorite!

If you were in the sky you
would be the brightest star,

but I am so glad you are
where you are, so I can
hold your hand and kiss
your face!

Because you are my favorite.

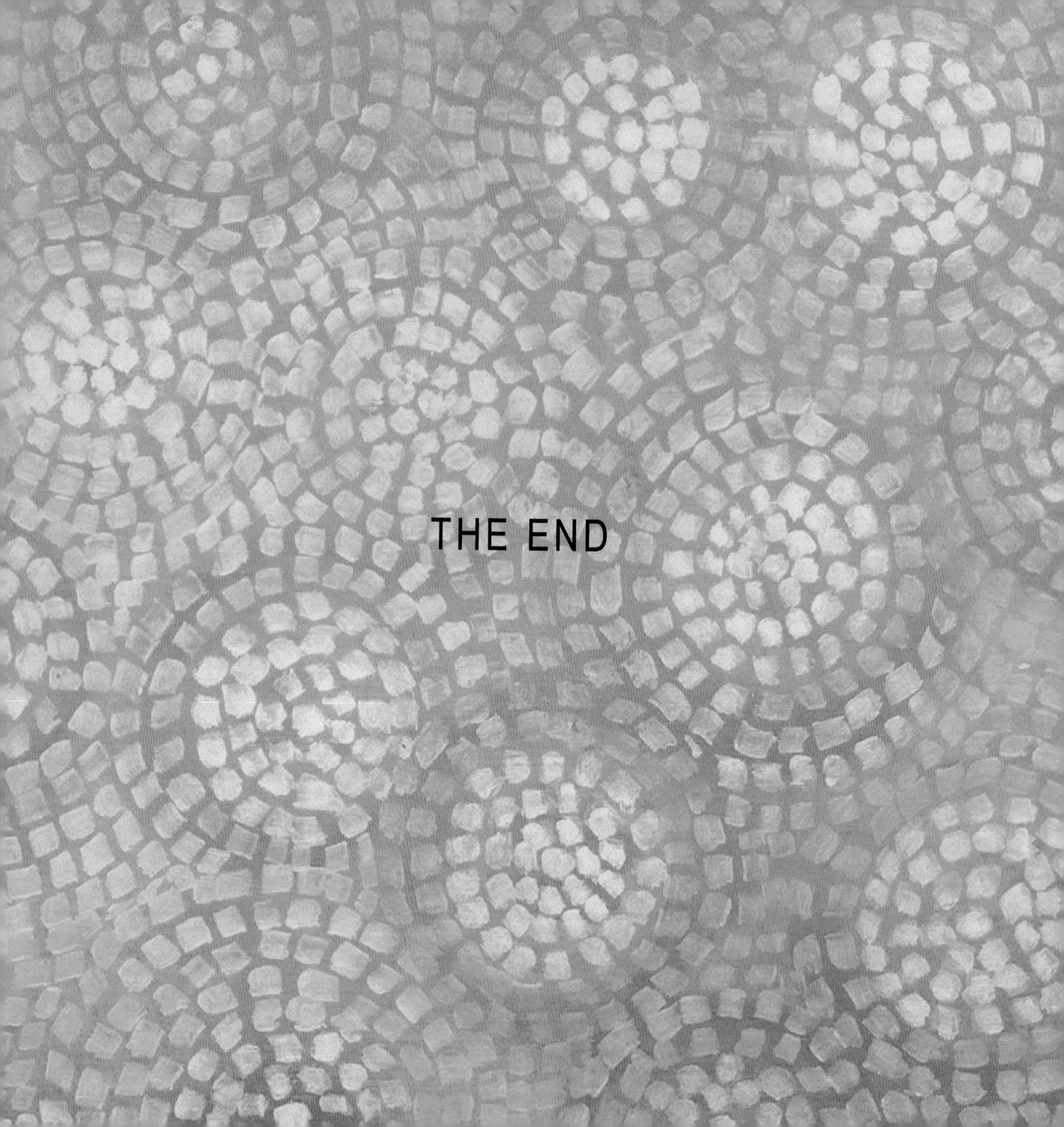

THE END

Made in the USA
Charleston, SC
21 July 2014